What Everybody Ought To Know About Lawn Care & Landscaping

Byrd's Lawn & Landscape's Guide To Getting Your Best Lawn Ever

Sam Byrd

Table Of Contents

My Story

Hello everyone, my name is Sam Byrd and I am the owner of Byrd's Lawn and Landscape LLC. located in Brevard County Florida. I am native to the State and was born and raised here in Brevard County.

Ever since I was a child I loved the outdoors. Whether it was sports, climbing trees, or just playing in the rain, I always looked forward to going outside. My dad was big into gardening and landscaping his back yard and that was my first step to growing a green thumb. He would have me help him lay mulch in the beds or put the plants into the ground. I caught on quick and at first it seemed like a chore, but as I matured I started to enjoy the gardening work with my father.

All the hard work we put in landscaping his backyard paid off because it was our little paradise back there. Years later after graduating high school my first job was my father's western store. While I was working at the family store I met a nice girl named Savannah. We seemed to click very well and started dating within a few weeks of working together. I enjoyed working for my dad but being cooped up inside all day just wasn't for me.

So, I ended up leaving and getting my second job at Ace Hardware. I liked the fact that I got to do it all from working in the plumbing section to filling up propane outside. I learned a lot working at ace and it kept me on my toes. But the issues I had with working there was the minimum hourly wage with no raises and still being stuck in retail still. I also did not like the fact that my hours and work days changed every week. I was at Ace for over two years. During these two years, Savannah and I were living at my mom's home. We really wanted to get a place of our own and move out to have a better life together.

We both were in college at the time and had part time jobs. With the minimum wage and part time hours I was getting there was no way we were going to be able to afford an apartment. So, I decided to do two things. First, I asked one of my good friends and coworker Cole if he would be interested in rooming with us in an apartment which he was. The second thing I decided to do was to start mowing my dad's store and 3 other family homes to make a little extra cash to pay the bills. My dad let me borrow his old run down residential John Deere mower and Stihl weed whacker. I bought a small gas-powered blower from ace also. Luckily, I already owned my own truck and had a small open trailer my neighbor sold to me for a good price.

Then I was cutting a few yards on my off day to make a couple hundred bucks so I could pay my rent. I enjoyed getting out there and mowing a few yards because I felt free and nice to not have to listen to a boss telling you what to do. Before I knew it, I was my family member's neighbors were coming over and asking for a price to mow their yard. I must have been doing a good job with the yard or maybe they just saw that I was a young entrepreneur trying to come up in the world and wanted to help.

Either way before I knew it I had 15 lawn accounts, which by myself only took one to two days to do and I was making just as much money doing those 15 yards as I was making all week at Ace Hardware. I started to think wow this is much better money and I really enjoy what I do. I came up with a plan when I acquired 20 yards I was going to leave ace and start mowing full time. That only took a few more months and I met my goal. I put in my two weeks and registered my lawn company through the State of Florida. I decided to call my business Byrd's Lawn and Landscape LLC. to keep the last name strong.

I also got insurance to be 100% legit. Before I knew it, I was hiring one of my friends on part time to help me out and the company started to get rolling. My grandpa is a true entrepreneur himself who made a very good living from his technology business saw that I was putting a lot of effort into my business and decided to help me out. He helped me purchase my first real commercial mowers.

With this huge opportunity I took the two mowers and ran with it. I had a professional copywriter and marketer named Austin Fraley who also runs his own personal training business and is a good friend help design and build up my own website and help market my business. I started asking my customers to leave reviews on my different business pages which helped tremendously. It has been over three years now since I started my company and we are booming. We now have over hundred accounts ranging from small residential homes to full size shopping centers. I have three full time employees that are great and together we work great as a team. And best of all I got married to my wife Savannah. The following years are only looking up and cannot wait to see what it brings. All it took was some motivation and a passion for success!

Here I wanted to distill some of the things I've learned over the years so you can get your best lawn ever. Enjoy!

A Home Made Solution To Getting Rid Of Those Pesky Weeds!

Alright let's be honest when it comes to yard work no one enjoys pulling weeds. I mean who wants so sit out there on their knees for hours on end pulling up each and every weed one by one. It's painful and can really take a toll on your body especially in the hot sun of the Space Coast.

There has to be a better way right?

Now I know you're probably thinking "Pull up weeds one by one? Who does that anymore I use chemicals from the store!" a seemingly easy for fix for a common problem. However there are many dangers of using store bought chemicals.

No one wants their pets, children, or other loved ones in a yard that has been infected with harmful chemicals that your typical lawn care company uses. Instead you want something that is going to be powerful enough to kill the weeds while at the same time not powerful enough to turn your yard into a radioactive wasteland in the process.

The natural weed killer solution.

With ingredients that can be found in your kitchen you can make your own formula for getting rid of those pesky weeds without compromising the safety of your family.

All you need is a spray bottle, dish soap, white distilled vinegar, and water. With this you can make your own powerful weed killing, lawn protecting, family saving formula. Plus it's much better than pulling them all out one by one.

Here are the steps to making your own weed killing formula.

Step #1

First get together all of the ingredients you'll need. You need to have a spray bottle, white distilled vinegar, dish soap, and a source of water.

Step #2

First fill up 2/3 of the spray bottle with white distilled vinegar.

Step #3

Then you are going to add in a couple of drops of dish soap. Dish soap is powerful you don't need to use a lot to get the results that you want.

Step #4

Then fill up the rest of the spray bottle with water and be sure to mix it thoroughly.

Step #5

Apply to weeds. This works best if done on a dry hot day so the solution can really soak in.

Warning! This solution will kill any plants that you spray it on as well so make sure to be selective with where you spray.

And there you have it a much preferable solution to getting rid of weeds than using dangerous chemicals or spending your time breaking your back pulling them all out one by one.

How To Get The Perfect Green Lawn

Everyone wants to have that perfect green lawn. You know the one I'm talking about. So green it nearly blinds you, lush, full, looks like the perfect place for the kids to play or have a BBQ on, yeah you know the one I'm talking about.

Most people think that lawns like that only exist on TV or in some high end neighborhood in Miami somewhere, but that is not true. By utilizing the tips outlined in this article you too can have a nice lush green lawn that is the envy of your neighbors and friends.

So let's get started.

So first off there are some common sense tasks that just have to be done. Your lawn must be mowed, watered, and fed regularly. This is the trifecta of having a good lawn. But there are some lesser known tips that can go far in giving you that perfect green lawn you desire.

Tip #1 – Mow Weekly

You must have your lawn mowed weekly, even if you feel like it doesn't need it. Now I know you're asking "Why is this?" and I'll be happy to tell you.

When your grass grows high it blocks out sun on the grass below it. Your grass needs to be exposed to sun in order to grow. If this sunlight is blocked off from trees, potted plants, or even having high grass and weeds it can die and lead to dead spots, which is something no one wants.

When you mow your lawn weekly you ensure that all that grass is getting adequate sunlight so that it can grow strong and stay green.

Tip #2 – Aerate The Soil

The foundation of having lush green grass is having grass that has strong and deep roots. Grass that has strong roots is able to grow better and stay healthier looking.

It is recommended that you aerate your lawn at least once a year. What aerating your lawn does is it helps loosen up the soil and get air into it. And this is important because that allows for water to get deep down into the grass and not just on a surface level.

This leads to stronger deeper roots which leads to a lusher greener grass stemming from those roots.

Tip #3 – Address Dead Spots

Dead spots are patches of your grass that are well dead. This can be from not getting enough sun, an animal tearing it up, a potted plant, insects or even a deadly fungus. However dead spots can be easily addressed.

For dead spots that are not caused by insects or fungus's all you need to do is get as many sq ft. of sod to completely replace the dead area, then cut dead grass out with shovel and replace with the new sod. The great thing about turf is that you can cut it into any shape needed.

Now for dead spots that are caused by insects like chinch bugs or white grubs or a grass fungal you will need to purchase a good granule or liquid insect and fungicide killer to spray or spread around the entire dead area. A couple applications of that should take care of this problem. If not you more than likely you will need to call a insecticide company to take care of the problem.

After cutting out the turf and placing it you are going to want to use a good fertilizer to give the new sod a boost. The best fertilizer to use is a strong high quality liquid fertilizer in brands like *Miracle-Gro* and *Scotts* to ensure the new turf gets all the nutrition's it needs to become established and healthy.

So there you have it, three simple tips that are sure to make your lawn the greenest it can be!

How To Properly Water Your Lawn

One of the greatest things about living on Florida's Space Coast is that we get plenty of sun and generally all year round. You know that the summers can be hot and even the winters can see weather in the 80's or higher. Because of this if you want to maintain your nice green lawns you need to make sure to make sure you are properly watering it.

Grass dies without water, we all know this. And in the constant exposure of the hot Florida sun proper watering of the yard is especially important. However with that we also get lots of rain, properly watering your yard is all about balance and will be explained below.

How Much Water

The first thing you need to know is how much water your lawn needs. On average the typical lawn needs between 1 and 1.5 inches of water weekly. Obviously things like drought can change this but 1 to 1.5 inches is a good baseline to start with, you can always adjust as needed.

For example if you're getting frequent showers then stick to 1 inch a week but if there hasn't been any rain and its hot then go for 1.5 inches of water a week.

How Do I Measure

So now that you know how much water you need the next logical question is how do I measure the amount of water my lawn is getting?

The answer to this is the rain gauge. They can be picked up at your local gardening/lawn care store. Once you have the rain gauge you are going to put it out in your yard in the center of your sprinklers "firing range".

You don't want it too close to the sprinkler but you don't want it too far either.

Then go ahead and run your sprinklers. Checking on the gauge periodically. When the gauge hits 1 inch or 1.5 depending on what you are going for you will know how much time you should run your sprinklers for weekly.

How Frequent Should I Water

Now that you know how long you need and how to measure the next thing you need to address is how often.

I recommend watering your lawn 2 to 3 times a week. You only want to water a half inch at a time. Otherwise the water isn't going to be absorbed. You want the watering to dry out before you do the next watering for maximal effect.

You do not want to water every single day, you will be wasting water and not helping your lawn. Do a half inch at a time to get to the weekly goal of 1-1.5 inches depending on weather conditions.

Don't worry about a little rain throwing off your measurements this doesn't have to be exact as long as you are in the ballpark you will be coming home to a nice fresh green lawn.

How To Fix Stubborn Brown Spots In Your Yard

No one likes brown spots in their yard. They look awful and are a eye sore to you and your neighbors. While laying sod is always an option sometimes it isn't enough and can be much more costly.

Some brown spots require more extensive work and involve working the soil itself. Otherwise you will simply be addressing the symptom of the problem and not the cause by laying down a layer of sod.

So here is how to address hard to cure brown spots in your yard.

Step #1 – Loosen The Soil

The first thing you want to do is loosen the soil on the brown spot. You'll want to rake the area with a hard rake to take out the dying and dead grass. This allows for new grass to grow and prevents a layer of dead grass from building up keeping your lawn from staying brown.

Step #2 – Lay Down A Starter Fertilizer

The next thing you want to do once the soil has been loosened and the dead grass raked away is lay down a starter fertilizer. You'll want to look on your starter fertilizer for three numbers. For example on the higher quality brands you'll see a rating of 12-24-11 or something close to those numbers.

This rating corresponds to the amounts of nitrogen, phosphorous, and pot ash respectively. The most important measurement we are looking for to address brown spots is the amount of phosphorous.

The reason for this is phosphorous promotes root growth.

Look for one with a high middle number and you're good to go.

Step #3 – Lay Seed

The next step is to pick the right grass seed for your yard and lay it down. For example for a shaded area you want grass seeds that grow well in shaded areas and so on and so forth. You want to be generous with laying down the seed.

It's better to put too much than to little seed just to be safe. After laying the seed you need to cover it with compost or a rich soil with nutrition's added. Make sure it's all covered with a light layer of fresh soil, compost, or manure because otherwise if the seed is exposed to the element it more than likely won't take.

After that you want to make sure you water the area good.

Step #4 – Give It Time

Give it a few weeks and your brown spot should have turned into a green spot and your yard should be looking great!

How To Effectively Spread Mulch

Mulching your yard is something that at first glance seems to be a no brainer. After all you just throw it around, make sure there isn't any bald spots, and then you're good to go right?

Not so fast!

Properly mulching your yard is a little more complicated than that and is very important for the health of your yard as well as its overall look and curb appeal.

There are ways not only to make sure your mulching looks good but also keeps your plants, trees, and grass healthy as well as things you need to do before you mulch to ensure you get the most out of it.

Before Your Mulch

Before you start mulching you are going to want to make sure that you have cleared out the majority of weeds and removed any dead leaves. While we don't have as much dead leaves down here in Florida, even a small amount is enough to hinder the effectiveness of your mulch.

Once you have the bed cleaned then you can bring out the bags of mulch.

How To Properly Mulch

First things first you must never pile up mulch more than three inches deep. When mulch gets above three inches it makes it hard for nutrients and rain to get into the soil and can actually harm your plants and trees.

You want to make sure the mulch has a relatively even spread and never goes above three inches in any one place. This includes along the base of trees and around shrubs. Mulch piling up can cause trees to rot and die as well as can kill of shrubs in addition to preventing nutrients and water getting into the soil.

Something that we definitely don't want!

Others Things To Keep In Mind

Something that you'll want to do when you have a layer of old mulch you are laying new mulch over is you need to turn your mulch. You want to get a garden weasel and run it along your bed turning your mulch.

You want to do this because old mulch (especially mulch with high wood content) they get so matted down that after being there for months they don't allow water through. When you turn it you break it up and allow the nutrients and water to get back through.

Now you know how to properly mulch your garden and can rest assured your mulching job will increase your curb appeal as well as the health of your plants, trees, and lawn.

How To Lay Sod Like A Pro

When done properly sod can make your yard look spectacular, the key word there being properly. To prevent your sod job looking like it was done by amateurs (even if it was) you need to know how to lay sod like a pro.

In this article you will learn the proper way to lay sod. The way the pros (like us here at Byrd's Lawn & Landscape!) do it so that you can turn a brown backyard into a lush green getaway.

So without further ado let's get started.

Step #1 – Get Rid Of The Old Grass

First things first you have to get rid of that old grass before you can put in the new. Don't lay sod over old grass, this is probably obvious to you but there are those who have tried. You want a fresh patch of dirt to work from. We recommend spraying the existing grass first with a good weed and grass killer to make removing the old grass a lot easier while at the same time killing off the weeds so they do not sprout and take over the new sod.

Step #2 – Loosen The Top Soil

It is very important to loosen up that top layer of soil so that when the sod is laid down the roots can take to the soil. If you don't loosen up the soil it is much harder for the roots to take and then your sod will die and we don't want that.

To loosen the soil go over it with a rotator or use an hard rake if a rotator is not an option. As long as those top few inches of dirt are loosened up you'll be just fine.

Step #3 – Lay Down Compost

The next thing you are going to want to do is lay down a layer of compost over the dirt. You want to make sure the compost is evenly laid so that your new sod will go down evenly as well. You are going to want to lay a one inch deep layer of compost, nothing higher than that.

Use a rake to spread out the compost and make sure it is evenly laid out.

Step #4 – Put Down The Sod

You want to lay your new sod in straight lines as best as you can. Simple place the sod starting at one end of the yard and then roll or throw it down to the other. Obviously there are times when a straight line isn't going to work but stick to it as much as you can for a clean looking job.

One thing to keep in mind is whenever two pieces of sod are placed together where they meet is called the seam. You want to push the seams together in the dirt. Otherwise the sod on the seam will dry out.

Step #4 – Maintain The Sod

Now that the sod is down you want to make sure it takes root and stays green. You want to water it every day for the first week and then you are going to reduce to half that for the second week. After the first 2 weeks stay within the 1-1.5 inches of water daily just like you would for any other part of your lawn

So there you have it, you now have the know how to lay sod like a pro!

Warning! You May Be Killing Your Trees With This Common Mulching Technique

Mulching around your tree when done improperly can lead to the death of the tree. Most lawn care businesses don't know this. Properly mulching your tree can be the difference between a healthy good looking tree that compliments your yard and a dead tree that you have to pay to get rid of and replace or spend your valuable time getting it out yourself.

Neither of which are great options. Instead when you know how to properly mulch around a tree you'll never have to worry about this again.

The Wrong Way

The first thing I'm going to talk about is the wrong way to mulch your tree. The way that will kill your tree and cost you lots of time and/or money. Not to mention this is the way that many landscaping companies do it.

This is called the "mulch volcano" way and it's where a landscaper will pile up a mound of mulch around your tree. Resembling a volcano with the spout being your tree. This is very bad for the tree and can kill it.

This is because this mound of mulch suffocates the tree's root mass and leads to it not getting the nutrients it needs. Which leads to the bark falling off and eventually death. Most landscapers don't know this and may be killing your trees!

If you ever see a mound of mulch around your tree it's time to hire another landscaper and save your trees.

The Right Way

So now that you know the wrong way what is the right way?

Once you have your mulch the first thing you want to do is spread it around the tree base. You don't want to just dump the wheelbarrow down but rather want to either shovel the mulch out or do it by hand for a more even displacement of the mulch.

Remember we don't want to use too much.

Also by doing it by hand you can better measure the depth. You never want to go higher than two inches, even at the base of the tree never go higher than two inches. Otherwise you will be damaging the tree.

Make sure that the mulch is evenly spread and doesn't go over two inches. With those two guidelines in mind you'll never have to worry about damaging your tree and have a properly done mulch job you can be proud of.

How To Get Rid Of Crab Grass

Crab grass is a pain. Not only does it ruin the look of your yard but it can also damage the grass around it. Killing off your good grass while making your lawn look worse, now that's something we definitely don't want.

Crab grass is something that affects lawns all over and Melbourne is no exception. Now I should point out that the best way to take care of crab grass is to prevent it in the first place. You know how the saying goes "an ounce of prevention is worth a pound of cure". To prevent crab grass you need to have a strong green lawn. One that is properly watered and has deep roots.

If you've been following the other lawn tips from Byrd's Lawn & Landscape you already got this covered. However there still may be the occasional crab grass sprouting and here is how you get rid of it.

Step #1 – Get Rid Of The Current Crab Grass

Crab grass seeds need sun to grow they cannot survive in the shade. When you have healthy green grass that is lush it naturally prevents it however when you do have it the first thing you need to do is get rid of it.

The best way to do this is to set your mower on the lowest setting possible and go over the crab grass. Warning! Only do this with a mower that has a bag otherwise you are going to be throwing the crab grass all over the yard making the infestation even worse.

Go over all the crab grass and then take the bag and dump it in a safe place away from your yard. Throw it in the trashcan or somewhere safe. Just not near or on your lawn (or the lawn of a neighbor).

Step #2 – Reseed The Lawn

Now you do not have to reseed your entire lawn, just where the crab grass was. This will prevent the crab grass from coming back and keep the crab grass seeds from taking. The first thing you need to do is lay down a layer of compost so that your seeds are going to take. Spread it out evenly where you are going to put the seeds.

After the compost you are as always going to want to throw down a layer of starter fertilizer. After the starter fertilizer is down then you are going to want to start laying the seed. Take a seeder and then give it a go over spreading the seed. Then take a rake and go over it with the back of a rake to bury the seed lightly.

Then water once per day for a week. Only lightly don't flood it which will upturn the seed and it can float away or get eaten.

There you have it. Something else you can do is put down a crab grass control. Also if you see any crab grass in your yard (one or two sometimes pop up no matter what) simply pull it out by hand (make sure to take out the roots) then throw it in the trash can.

How To Plant A Tree The Right Way

There are a variety of trees to pick from and before you go about planting it the first thing you need to do is understand the typical height and width of the tree you want to plant. You need to make sure there is going to be room and that there aren't things that could cause a problem down the road, such as power lines or planting a large tree too close to your house.

Once you have that down you are ready to go and plant it. So you have your tree picked out, you know the typical height and width. You have measured to make sure where you want to plant it will work out. And you have made note of any problems such as power lines or it being too close to the house. Now you're ready to plant your tree.

Step #1 – Measure The Width Of The Receiving Hole

The first thing you want to do is put down a stake where you want to put the tree. You are going to want the receiving hole to be twice the diameter of the tree's root ball (the base that's wrapped if it came from a nursery). Use a tape measure to measure from the stake and mark off where you have to dig to.

Then do to the other side. Now you have the markings of where your receiving hole is going to end. Then once that markings are put down you want to strip the grass in the area where the hole is going to go.

You can use an iron rake, a shovel, or a pick. All can work though an iron rake is going to be your best bet. Also never forget to call your local utility company to make sure you aren't going to hit anything important or dangerous.

Step #2 – Measure The Depth Of The Receiving Hole

The next thing you need to do is figure out how deep you are going to have to dig you're receiving hole. You need to measure the base of the tree. You want to make sure that the root flare (where the roots spread out at, generally two or so inches below the trunk) is below ground.

You also don't want to bury the trunk. So measure the base and then dig the requisite amount. You might want to shave off an inch or two from the total base measurement so that the trunk does get buried.

Now that you have your measurement you are going to start digging. You want to make sure that the hole is even where you are going to put the tree in. If it goes up on the sides a little bit that's no big deal. But you want a level surface where the tree will be sitting.

Step #3 – Plant The Tree

Put the tree base in the hole. Simple enough. Make sure that it is centered in the role. Roll it so that it is. Next make sure the tree is sitting evenly. You may want to put some soil on one side if it is leaning to one side. This is very important you don't want your tree to grow in any direction but straight up and down.

Remove whatever that has covered the root ball and throw it away. You then want to loosen the roots up. You can do this with your hands or with a handheld cultivator. You are also going to want to remove any roots that are wrapping around the trunk of the tree. If they aren't taken care of then they will harm the growth of the tree.

You then want to fill in the hole with a mix of the soil you dug up, compost, and start fertilizer. This ensures that the tree is going to get all the nutrients that it needs to take root and grow healthily. After the hole is filled in you are going to want to water the tree. Really soak the entire area.

And there you have it. You now have a tree that will grow to provide shade for your family and add beauty to your yard for years to come!

How To Sharpen Your Lawn Mower Blades

You may have never thought about sharpening your lawn mower blades before. Many don't. However if you want to get the most out of your mower as well as have a healthy lawn you need to periodically sharpen your blade.

If you don't sharpen your blade your lawn will have an uneven cut as well as with using ragged blades can introduce disease into your yard killing it. You need to keep your blades sharp and ready to go.

As long as you aren't hitting rocks, dirt, or other debris all the time you really only need to sharpen your blades about 3-4 times during the growing season and you'll be solid. However if you hit a rock you need to sharpen it right away.

First Remove The Blades

Now this is really going to depend on what type of mower you are using and I would refer you to the instructional manual that came with your particular mower. However with that being said there are some things to keep in mind that can make this a lot easier for you.

For safety purposes you want to make sure you are removing the mower's spark plug. That way there is no way the engine can fire. Also you want to make sure that you are using the right size socket for the nuts otherwise you could round them off and then you're really screwed. Also you'll want to keep the blades in place with a glove instead of a wood piece which can bend it.

Sharpen The Blades

Now there are a couple of different methods you can use to sharpen your blade the vary with their effectiveness. The first is to simply use a metal file. Put the blade in a vise and then simply run the file along the edge of the blade until sharp. Think sharpening a knife like in the boy scouts.

The next thing you can use is a cordless drill with a sharpening stone attachment with a plastic guide. All you have to do with that is run the guide along the blade and your good to go. Much easier than the file and more effective as well. Well worth the investment.

However the easiest way of them all is to use a bench grinder. If you have a bench grinder then this is what you are going to want to use. Simply run the blade along the grinder until sharp. Simple and easy. It doesn't take long! If you do not have a bench grinder you can use an angle grinder to sharpen the blade and a bench vise to hold the blade. Make sure to sharpen the edge at a 15 degree angle.

Balance

Now you want to make sure that the blade is balanced. To do this simply find a nail on the wall (or put one there) and place the blade on it. Generally the blade is going to fall to one side or the other. You'll know that whichever side it falls to needs to have more metal removed (sharpened longer) so that it's balanced.

You don't have to get this perfect but having a very uneven blade can result in damage to your mower as well as a shoddy mowing job, two things that no one wants. Once both sides are reasonably close you are good to go.

Are You Making These 3 Lawn Mowing Mistakes?

Mowing your lawn at first glance might seem to be pretty simple. I mean after all it's just running over your grass with a machine until it's not so long right? While on the surface it may seem simple there is actually a lot that goes into mowing your lawn properly.

Many homeowners and even other lawn companies make these mistakes that can tear up your lawn and ruin your yard. These mistakes are some of the most common we've seen and we can always tell when we get a new yard if the previous lawn company had been making them.

Follow this guide to avoiding these common lawn mowing mistakes so that you can keep your lawn healthy and green all year long!

Mistake #1 – Not Keeping Your Lawn Blades Sharp

A common mistake and one that results with a lawn that doesn't get cut but gets torn up and literally. When your lawn blades aren't consistently sharpened they end up tearing out grass instead of cutting it. Then you end up with a patchy lawn or with a lawn with brown tips. Both undesirable outcomes that no one wants.

You want to keep your lawn blades sharp with consistent sharpening of 3-4 times during the growing season and then probably at least one other time during the year. Also if you hit any rocks or large sticks during mowing you need to sharpen your blades.

Mistake #2 – Cutting Your Lawn Too Short

Many people have asked what the proper height is for their grass. While this will very from grass to grass so there is no set height but you can go based of a measurement. When cutting your grass you never want to cut off more than 1/3 of the grass. Make sure your mower height is adequate to do this otherwise you will be cutting too short and harming your grass.

Cutting your lawn too short can hurt the root system and prevent it from growing deep. Which will result in a patchy brown lawn from the grass dying. Remember root depth is a good indicator of grass health and therefore if you want a green lush lawn you must have grass with deep roots. So only cut the top 1/3 off, never more.

Mistake #3 – Not Cleaning The Lawn Before Hand

Before you mow you have to make sure your lawn is clear. What do I mean by this? Before mowing you are going to want to go through your lawn and make sure to pick up any large rocks or sticks that could damage your mower's blades.

This is especially important right after a storm (especially a hurricane!) so that you don't clog your mower up with stuff it can't cut properly. One rock can ruin your mower's blades and even the mower if it big enough. So make sure that the area you are going to mow is free of any debris that could damage your mower.

Summary

So there you have it three mistakes that most mowers make but are easily avoidable.

How To Mow An Overgrown Lawn

Vacation, heavy rains, life. From time to time we aren't able to give our lawns the care and frequent cuttings that they need (unless of course we hire a great lawn team like us at Byrd's Lawn & Landscape). When this happens our grass can become overgrown and a bit unruly.

However don't just charge out with your mower going at it. There are a couple things you want to keep in mind when you mow an overgrown lawn so that it turns out alright and looks good once it has been cut down to its normal length.

Step #1 – Raise Your Mower

You don't want to keep your mower at its normal height when mowing an overgrown lawn. This is going to cause you some issues as well as may cut your grass too short. Remember you generally only want to cut about 1/3 of the grass at the time to prevent damage. An overgrown lawn is an example when you go a bit more than this but don't go too crazy.

You are going to want to raise your mower up to its maximal height so that you can get a good even cut across your lawn without cutting it too deep and damaging the grass. Just because the grass is taller does not necessarily mean its stronger so you still have to treat it right just like you would if it was at its normal height.

Step #2 – No Mulching

If you have a mulch plug you are going to want to take it out. While it can be good to do mulching often you are just going to want to bag it for an overgrown lawn. The reason for this is that because the grass is so high it may clump up if we keep the mulch plug in.

Obviously this is something that we want to prevent so just use the bag for now. The bag is going to be able to take the high volume of grass that is going to becoming in without slowing down and keep you on track for getting your lawn tamed once again.

Step #3 – Mow

The step is pretty self-explanatory. Go ahead and mow just like you usually would. Go in one direction (north/south, east/west, etc.). Remember you mower should be on its highest setting at this point not its normal one.

Step #4 – Set Back Down To Normal Height And Mow Again

Now you are going to set your mower back down to its normal height and you going to mow the yard again. However this time you are going to mow in the opposite direction that you mowed in before. So if you mowed from north to south before this time you are going to mow from east to west.

So there you have it. A bit of work but worth it to make sure your yard stays healthy and green even if it's been neglected for a little bit.

How To Make Your Lawn Crazy Green Through Science!

Alright so you want a green lawn, and I mean a green lawn. A lawn so green that it shines. Alright so maybe green doesn't shine but you get the point. You want a blindingly green lawn. Well this is a possibility for all but the most unhealthy of lawns.

Green grass is for the most part healthy grass. So it makes sense that to have green grass you should be following all of the lawn tips here at Byrd's Lawn & Landscape. Proper lawn care (the kind we do here at Byrd's

Lawn & Landscape) is the foundation of a green lawn. But once you understand that there are certain "hacks" you can use to make it even greener.

That is where science comes in!

What Makes A Lawn Green?

So first off what is it that makes a lawn green? Well we already said healthy grass but its gets a little more technical than that. It's going to come down to two chemicals and those chemicals are nitrogen and iron.

Nitrogen is the main chemical that makes a lawn green and this comes from photosynthesis which turns sunlight into sugars which feeds the grass. Pretty cool right? Anyways a green lawn is one that is properly photosynthesizing. And having the right amount of nitrogen is key in ensuring good photosynthesis and a green healthy lawn!

Iron also plays a role in making your yard green and supporting good photosynthesis. Now while nitrogen is generally found in pretty healthy amounts in most yards iron is a little more complicated. Many yards lack proper iron content and therefore to get the crazy green look we're going for you need to add iron.

Adding In Iron

You are going to want to put down an iron that is "chelated" what this means is that the iron is ready for absorption. So you know the grass is going to take the iron because it's already broken down. Otherwise you could be spreading iron that isn't going to take to the soil and isn't going to do anything for your lawn.

You are going to want to use an organic solution of chelated iron because the organic solution slowly releases (unlike the non-organic which goes all at once) and prevents you from putting too much iron in your yard which can be harmful to it and turn your lawn grey.

Then throw the mix in a spreader and go and spread it. Your lawn will be green in no time.

Also as a side tip there are mixtures that contain nitrogen as well if your lawn is low.

How To Ruin A Perfectly Good Yard By Working Too Hard

Most are under the impression that they have to mow their lawn every week or it will look poor and be unhealthy. However the reality is a little more complicated than that. Mowing frequency is determined more by grass height and growth than it is by time.

For example mowing every week during the colder months will end up killing your grass and mowing every other week during the spring months could not be enough...or could it?

Most people mow their lawn every week out of habit. It doesn't matter if the grass has grown to three inches or only an inch long. However getting out there and mowing every week could be killing your grass. Let me explain why.

Proper Height

You want your grass to be about 2 1/2 inches during the cooler months and even as tall as 3 inches during the hot summer months. Now obviously depending on what type of grass you have this may change a little bit but these are good numbers to go off of.

Healthy green grass is grass with deep healthy roots. If you cut your grass more than 1/3 of its height or cut it too frequently it hurts your grass which impacts the root depth. Short grass cannot grow deep roots. If you continually mow your grass to an inch its roots will never get a chance to grow deep and your grass will be unhealthy because of that.

When your grass doesn't have deep roots it allows disease to get in, weeds to grow, and the grass to die which causes patches and brown spots. If you see a yard with lots of brown patches as well as many weeds it is a good bet that the grass was never able to develop deep roots and died because of it.

Mow For Height Not Time

You want to make sure you are mowing for height and not for time. Many times this will end up being either every week or every other week. But not always. Its important to not let your grass be mowed down too short or it will never take root and you will end up with an ugly brown yard.

Allow the grass to grow. Never cut it down to an inch. Never mow more than 1/3 of the grass's full height at any one time. Take measurements every now and then just to make sure that you're not cutting it too short and follow the rest of the lawn tips at Byrd's Lawn & Landscape and you'll be good to go!

So make sure you're not working too hard, it might be bad for your grass.

How To Edge Your Lawn With A String Trimmer

If you want a yard that really pops and makes your house look spectacular you need to make sure that you are edging and that you are doing so properly. While you can use an edger (such as the ones we use here at Byrd's Lawn & Landscape) not everyone can afford one and so they need to edge using different methods.

While not everyone has an edger pretty much every does have a string trimmer (weed whacker). What most don't know is that you can do halfway decent edging job with a string trimmer if you know how to do it right. In this article here we are going to lay out how to properly edge your lawn using nothing more than your basic string trimmer.

Things To Keep In Mind

When using a string trimmer when you edge your lawn you need to make sure that you are going to be running the string along the sidewalk at a 90 degree angle. There are many ways to do this. You can hold it with the mower up near your shoulder or whatever variation is easiest for you.

As long as those strings are going to be going at a 90 degree angle you are going to be good. Another thing you want to keep in mind is where the debris from the edging job is going to go. You can edge from either side just keep in mind if you recently cleaned up your sidewalk or driveway you want to do it at an angle that is going to fling dirt, mud, and grass all over it.

Start Edging

To edge you are simply going to run the string trimmer along the side of your sidewalk and driveway. Keep it at a 90 degree angle as you go down to get an even and consistent level. Don't go too fast, keep an even slow and steady pace and you'll end up with a good edging job and a great looking yard.

As you edge more and more it gets easier. Having an edge in place makes the next edging job even easier. So if your yard hasn't been edged before the first time will be the hardest. But once it's in place it'll get quicker and quicker every time you do it. A string trimmer won't provide you the same clean cut that an edger will but it can still do a great job and you won't have to spend your hard earned money on another tool.

So there you have a simple and cheap way to edge your yard without paying out money for extra equipment.

How To De-Thatch Your Lawn

Having a lawn that is filled with thatch will kill your grass and turn your green lawn brown. Over time any organic material that falls into your yard such as leaves, dead grass, roots, and anything else that has fallen onto your lawn and been broken down. What this does is form a layer over the soil that blocks nutrients from getting into your grass and plants.

Remember a green yard is a healthy yard. A yard that has a layer of thatch preventing your grass from getting the nutrients it needs is well on its way to being a brown eye sore. Another problem with thatch is that you can't reach it with a regular rake but need a special rake to even reach it. So now that you know how bad thatch is, it's time to learn how to address it and save your lawn from becoming a wasteland.

How To Get Rid Of Thatch

The first thing you need to do is ditch your traditional rake and instead use a specialized thatch rake for this job. A thatch rake has a row of sharpened half circles at the end that are specifically made to really get in the dirt and rip out that layer of unhealthy thatch. You want to run the thatch rake over your yard just like you would a regular rake.

Doing this is going to open up the lawn and allow for nutrients to get back into your grass keeping it green and healthy. When you are raking up the thatch you want to make sure that you aren't leaving any spaces because if you miss any you will end up with brown spots. Overlap where you rake to ensure that every inch of thatch is taken out and your grass can grow healthily.

How To Prevent Thatch

Now that you know how to handle a thatch filled yard the next problem is how to prevent it in the first place. Here are some things to keep in mind to prevent the buildup of thatch in your yard. First off make sure you are following of the lawn tips provided here at Byrd's Lawn & Landscape or even better using our services. Proper lawn care is the first line of defense against thatch building up in the yard.

In addition to following good lawn care tips such as proper watering and mowing your lawn frequently (but not too frequently) the next most important step is to have your soil aerated every now and then. How often depends on where you live but everyone should have their soil aerated at least once a year in some places more than that. Again it depends on where you live but it is essential for having a thatch free yard.

Alright now you know how to not only de-thatch your lawn but how to prevent thatch buildup in the first place.

How To Make Your Very Own Compost

You've probably heard about composting before. Composting is using just about any organic matter (with the exception of meat, cheese, and bread) you would usually throw in the trash and instead turning it into useful fertilizer. Composting is best done outdoors and can be an easy efficient way to get some very nutrient rich fertilizer for a garden bed or for trouble sections of your yard. Plus it's good for the environment.

So, let's get started!

Step #1 – Select A Container

You are going to want a container that can one last outside for a long period of time and two is big enough to hold quite a bit of "waste". A popular choice is a plastic trash can that you can get from the store. Other people use plastic bins as well. Choose whatever works best for you and fits in some part of your yard.

Step #2 – What To Put In The Container

Your compost container is going to need two things to provide you with the nutrient rich fertilizer that you can then use for your flower beds or garden. These two things are browns and greens. Browns are dead tree matter such as leaves and bark while greens are things like fruits, vegetables, and coffee grounds. You want about an even amount of each both are needed for your compost to come out healthy. You can also put grass clipping and egg shells in your compost.

Step #3 – Fill The Bottom

The first thing you want to do is form a bottom layer of twigs and straw to aerate your compost. Then after that you are going to want add a even mix of browns and greens into the mix. Whenever you have green scraps from the kitchen take them out to the compost and then mix it in with some leaves or twigs. As long as the compost stays relatively balanced it will begin forming into the nutrient rich stuff we want.

Step #4 – Maintain The Compost

You want to make sure that your compost doesn't dry out and isn't too exposed to the elements. If you are having heavy rains or other weather that could affect the compost then cover it up with something so that it maintains the state it needs. Also if it has been particularly dry and your compost is losing its moisture then water it to make sure it doesn't dry up on you.

Step #5 – Harvest Compost

After about three months your compost is going to be ready for use (if you've followed all the previous steps properly). You will know it is ready by the color, smell, and feel. It will start giving off an "earthy" smell, be dark brown, and is warm to the touch. It will be warm to the touch from all the healthy microbes in the soil. Once it has met these three criteria then it is ready to be used as an additive to the soil.

There you have, a great way to turn trash into nutrient rich fertilizer great for our gardens.

How Much Fertilizer Should I Use On My Lawn?

A common question that many lawn owners ask is "How much fertilizer should I put on my lawn?". While the exact amount is going to change depending on your lawn, the time of year, and many other factors there are some general guidelines that you can follow to ensure you have a healthy green lawn all year around.

One thing you want to avoid is over fertilizing the lawn which can be even more damaging to your lawn. Not fertilizing can prevent some growth and you may end with a yard that's not quite as lush as you want. However if you over fertilizer the lawn you can end up ruining your soil and messing up your grass's root system. Two things we don't want and that lead to dead brown lawns.

Don't Make This Common Mistake

The first thing that most lawn owners do is look at the back of the fertilizer bag which has a rough estimate of how much you are supposed to put down. However there are some issues with these measurements. For one you cannot known what spreader that they used and how it compares to your own. Some spreaders vary quite widely and so what worked for their spreader may be too much or too little for your own lawn.

The Proper Way

The first thing you want to do to properly fertilize your lawn is measure it. If you don't measure it then you will never know how much fertilizer is going to be required. Measure the length and the width to get the square footage of your lawn. Use a tape measure to make sure that it's accurate you don't want to estimate with these measurements as they could throw your fertilizer numbers off.

The next thing you want to do is look at your fertilizer and see how many square feet it says that it will cover and how much the bag actually weighs. Then divide the poundage of the bag by the square footage it covers (it easiest to do this by the thousands.

For example let's say that your lawn is 2,000 square feet. Now let's say the bag weights 45 lbs and covers 2,500 square feet. So we divide the bag weight by 2.5 (for the square footage it covers) and that will give us 18. So we know we need to spread 18 lbs of fertilizer for every one thousand square feet of the lawn.

Then multiple the total square footage of the yard (in thousands) by the number we just got. So it will be 2.0 X 18 which comes out to

36. So we know we will need to spread 36 lbs of the fertilizer to cover the yard properly.

It's a little complicated but worth it in the long run.

Why You Should Never Have Your Trees Topped

Tree topping refers to the practice of removing the entire tip off a tree (as opposed to trimming which is cutting of certain sections of the tree and improves its health). It is something that many own homers are convinced (either by unscrupulous lawn companies trying to make a buck or bad information through TV, internet, or other media source) will help the look of the yard.

However the reality of tree topping is very different. While it may sound nice to have all those annoying branches away from your house and tree topping may seem like an easy solution. The truth of the matter is tree topping is never the right option and in this article I am going to tell you why.

Why You Should Never Top A Tree

So you're looking out at your yard that you spend your time and money on trying to make it look nice. And there way up high is that pesky tree blocking sunlight from getting into your yard which makes the grass die and its branches are scrapping the roof making for a hazardous situation should high winds come.

So you ask around and someone recommends "Why not just have it topped. Simple, easily done. And will solve your problem quickly.". So you go and have your tree topped thinking "Great an easy, simple solution to my problem". But there's one problem. While at first you may be happy to have your problem solved you now realize you have an even bigger one.

The tree that was topped. One looks absolutely awful and unnatural. Sure the branches are gone but you didn't think the beauty of your yard would go with them. Then your tree begins dying off. So you throw tons of money at solutions trying to have it saved. However you are just left with a dead tree in your yard. Talk about an eye sore (and an expensive one to get removed).

What To Do Instead

If you have a tree that is overshadowing your yard or branches that are dangerously close to your house then you need to do something to resolve it. Both for the safety of your family and the beauty of your yard. However topping is never the answer.

Instead it is best to have it pruned. Now while pruning may be more expensive then topping (at first) over the long haul pruning is much safer, cheaper, and healthy for your tree. Pay the little extra money that a reputable lawn service will ask for pruning and you will have you yard back in shape in no time. Not to mention a tree that is safe and beautiful.

If someone ever agrees to top your tree run the other way. They are out to make a dollar and don't have the interest of your yard and you at heart. Topping is a cheap "solution" that never pans out how they tell you. Stick with pruning and you'll always have healthy trees that add to your yard.

3 Reasons You Should Use Topdressing In Your Lawn

Topdressing is the process of applying mix of soil and compost to your lawn to improve the health and look. While topdressing isn't generally used by the general public (though it should be) it has been used by golf course field managers as well as those that have to maintain athletic fields in top conditions. Such as practice fields at universities.

However you don't have to work at a top ten university or own a golf course to get benefits from topdressing your lawn. It can be done by the average home owner just like you. If you want a lush green healthy lawn that you and your family love and enjoy (not to mention raises your property value) then keep reading on for all the benefits of topdressing your lawn.

Reason #1 – Topdressing Makes Your Lawn Greener

A green lawn is for the most part a healthy lawn. Topdressing is a mix of soil and compost which adds much needed nutrients to you lawn resulting in better lawn health. The healthier your lawn is the greener it is going to be. In particular topdressing your lawn is going to add nitrogen to the lawn which is one of the main chemicals responsible for making your lawn lush and green.

Reason #2 – Topdressing Improves The Nutrients In Your Soil

You can't have good grass without good soil. Just like a building will fall part without a solid foundation, your grass will die without the solid foundation of good healthy soil. Topdressing uses the right mix of soil and compost that is required for grass to grow tall and full. Topdressing works great on areas that are resistant to grass growing such as areas with clay or that are rocky.

Reason #3 – Prevents Thatch Buildup

No one wants a lawn filled with thatch that ruins the look and health of your yard. With the application of topdressing you can help prevent the buildup of thatch. The materials used in topdressing eventually become part of your yard's soil. When using quality topdressing this will improve the grade of your soil and help with thatch breakdown.

So there you have it, three reasons to use topdressing in your yard. Topdressing while expensive only needs to be done every couple of years (of course this number varies depending on a number of factors) and can be just what your yard needs to take it to the next level.

How To Prune A Palm Tree

If there's one thing that stands out about Florida (and Brevard is no exception) it's the number of palm trees. Whenever someone sees an image of a palm tree the first thing that's going to pop into their mind is generally going to be sandy beaches, Pina coladas and of course Florida!

Palm trees when properly taken care off look wonderful and give you that vacation feel that you always want in a backyard. Who doesn't want to lay out in their hammock or on their patio and watch the gentle Space Coast winds drift through the palms. I know I do!

However just like any other tree to be healthy and look their best palm trees have to be pruned and pruned properly. Follow these easy steps lain out in this guide and you'll have wonderful looking palm trees all year long.

Step One – Determining If Your Palm Tree Needs To Be Pruned

Over pruning of a tree is just as damaging as not pruning it at all. You have to make sure before you get out your pole saw and ladder that your tree is actually in need of a trimming. Are there a bunch of dead fronds hanging off as well as dying palms all around it? If so then your tree is definitely in need of a pruning.

However if there is only one or two dead fronds feel free to peel them off but don't go overboard cutting off anything that you think might be a little bit unhealthy or just for aesthetic reasons. That could end up in hurting your palm tree or even killing it if done to an extreme, which will result in a costly removal as well as ruining the aesthetics of your yard. Two things we don't want.

Step Two – Use Your Hands

Before you start cutting you want to feel around the palm tree and break off anything that gives with a slight tug. You want to do this before you start cutting as it'll save you a lot of time as well as it's much easier then sawing off things that will give with a slight tug.

If it looks unhealthy give it a tug. If it comes off part way then you may be better off finishing it off with a saw but if it comes off almost completely go ahead and toss it aside.

Step Three – Cut Off The Dead

If a frond is brown, over dried, or diseased then it's coming off. Go ahead and get the pole saw and saw it off near the base. If a palm is drooping and seems like it'll fall off in a matter of time then go ahead and saw it off as well. However make sure you leave all the green upright palms alone. Cutting those down is bad for your tree.

At the end all the low hanging fronds that were dead or dying should be gone and you'll be left with a green upright palm tree. The king you'd expect to see in a commercial for a Florida resort or on a rum bottle.

Summary

And that's that. We here on Florida's Space Coast are lucky to be able to have such beautiful and wonderful trees right in our own backyards! Making a vacation only a few feet away.

How To Cut Down Large Branches Safely

For regular pruning of shrubs and small trees not much is required. As long as you know the basics and don't cut it down too much you're not going to do much damage. As a matter of fact about the worst damage you could do would be to the look of your yard. However when you move up a level and want to trim your oaks and other large trees that's when you run into trouble.

Cutting down a large branch improperly could result in it crashing down onto your fence, roof, or even you! It pays to have professionals (like us at Byrd's Lawn & Landscape: Brevard's #1 source for quality tree trimming) do it for you. Tree branches weigh a ton (sometimes literally) and add that to the falling from quite a height and you have a dangerous mix.

However if you're left without options then it's best to know how to cut down large branches, the safe way.

Step One – Start With The Undercut

The first thing you are going to want to do is start cutting on the underside of the branch. The initial cut should be away from where the branch meets the trunk. You are going to saw upwards until you are about half way through the branch. Be sure to not go higher than this as this will interfere with steps down the line and make the job much harder than it needs to be.

Step Two – Now With The Overcut

The next thing you are going to do is move up about 1-2 inches from where your undercut was (of course you're on the top side of the branch now) and begin sawing down. You are going to cut about half way down with the overcut as well. Now what's going to happen is the branch is going to begin falling off and the weight of the branch will tear it away from the tree naturally. You'll be left with a little stump.

Step Three – Cut The Stump

Now that the main mass of the branch has been dealt with without hurting the tree it's time to get rid of the remaining stump of the branch. Make a clean cut angling away from the trunk to remove the stump. You want to use this angle so that rain can naturally drain off the side and keep your tree healthy and looking good.

Step Four – Dispose Of Debris

The next thing you need to do is get rid of the debris around the yard. Depending on the size of the job you may want to take it too the dump or call a service (such as Byrd's Lawn & Landscaping) to haul it away for you, saving you the time and trouble of dragging the branches around and loading them up.

So there you have it, the easy and safe way to trim a tree.

How To Prune A Rose Bush

The rose symbolizes many things. Love, passion ,Valentine's day and perhaps most important of all a good looking garden that raises your home's value. However roses aren't going to look great on their own, they require care and maintenance.

To keep your roses looking good all year long you need to make sure you are pruning it right so that it can grow healthily. Like anything else when done properly roses can add value to your lawn as well as make your garden look beautiful. However when not taken care off they die or become misshapen and then you have to dig them up and get rid of them. Which is no fun for anyone.

So here is how you properly prune your rose bushes to keep them looking great all year long.

Note: This should be done in January or February for best effect. And make sure to wear long sleeve and gloves, roses can get nasty!

Step One – Remove All The Leaves

The first thing that you want to do before actually pruning your rose bush is remove all the leaves off the bush. While this may seem like it would harm your bush in reality it's good for it and allows for you to get a good look at what you are pruning. That way you can know you are pruning the right things and getting a good shape.

Step Two – Start Pruning

What you want to look for when you're pruning is any canes that are going towards the center of the plant or crossing with another cane. You also want to cut down anything that is diseased or dead obviously. You will know if a cane is dead by cutting into it. If it's brown then it's dead and if it's green then it's still alive. Just take off a little piece for testing and then if it's brown cut off the whole thing. Always make sure to cut at a 45 degree angle away from the bud so that rain can fall off it naturally.

Summary

There you have it. You should always prune your roses in winter to make sure that they'll stay healthy and look good all year long. The best way to ensure this is to follow the steps above and make you prune them good during the winter months.

How To Clean Up After A Hurricane

We living here on Florida's Space Coast are familiar with the damages hurricanes can cause. From 2004 when we were hit with Charley, Francis, & Jeanne to the more recent hurricane Matthew. Cleanup can be costly and at times dangerous.

In this article we are going to talk about the best ways to clean up after a hurricane both in efficiency and safety. First things first. No matter what with big things such as downed trees or large debris you may be better off hiring professionals to deal with it (such as us here at Byrd's Lawn & Landscape) mostly for safety concerns.

But with that being said there is still much you can do to get your yard in top shape after the storm has passed.

Prevention Is The Best Medicine

If you hear news about a major hurricane on the horizon (or right before hurricane season) is good time to have your trees trimmed and anything you think might become a problem removed. It's also a good time to make sure that your gutters are cleaned and that anything you want planted has been planted and had time to take root.

The start of hurricane season is a good time to have this all done. The planting, tree trimming, and everything else. That way it'll minimize the amount of damage and debris that'll be caused to your yard and home.

Clean Up The Small Stuff

Sticks and debris can be placed in trash cans and brought out to the trash. Leaves and smaller debris can be raked up and also placed in trash cans. Larger branches can be stacked up near wherever your trash is normally piled up. The only problem is it could take weeks or more before it's taken up.

Which means you'll have a pile of wood outside your home for some time. Not only does this look bad but it is also the perfect place for pests including dangerous spiders and snakes. To get it off right away you can call us (321-412-3006) and we'll be happy to remove all debris . Otherwise the city will eventually get it.

Large Debris

For large debris you want to be careful especially if it's tangled up in things. For example if it's tangled up in power lines even if it's on your property have the city or professionals get rid of it. You also want to be careful cutting up large fallen trees especially in the conditions after a hurricane.

This is another situation where you may be better off giving us a call (321-412-3006) and have us take care of it. But it's up to you. You can cut it up with a chainsaw and haul it away. Just remember to always use caution when doing so.

2 Ways To Get Rid Of Those Annoying Ants

Ants are annoying. They get in your home, pollute your food with their germs, and bite you when you're out trying to enjoy your lawn. You can try many different ways to get rid of them but not all work. Some work but are very expensive and others kill the ants but fail to completely stop them because they don't kill the queen.

In this article I am going to show you two simple ways you can get rid of those annoying ants once and for all. They don't require expensive chemicals or poison that you buy at the local hardware store and risk having your children or pets harmed but rather use things you can find in your kitchen or pickup from the store.

First the best way to keep ants out is prevention. You've probably heard the phrase and ounce of prevention is worth a pound of cure and that applies here as well. The best way to get rid of ants is having a healthy yard that is mowed and tended too regularly. You can do this yourself or hire us here at Byrd's Lawn & Landscape. Just so long as your yard is tended too frequently and is healthy.

Now for the methods.

Method #1 – Boiling Water

The first method is very simple and something anyone can do (of course use caution!). Simple get a pot and fill it full of water. Then boil that water. What you are going to do is pour the boiling water into the entrance way (the hole) at the top of the ant hill.

What this is going to do is get down in the hill to kill both the queen and all the larvae.

Works much better than poison that only kills the workers or poisons the top of the ant hill which does nothing to kill the queen or larvae which is the lifeblood of the hill.

Method #2 – Corn Meal Mix

Here's is what you're going to do. You are going to make a mixture of 2 teaspoons of cornmeal, 1 teaspoon of sugar, and 1 teaspoon of borax into a mixture. The cornmeal is for the ants to take the queen, the sugar is to bring them to it, and the borax is to kill them. Place this on the top of their hill.

Keep pets and children away from this. Because of the sugar in the mixture the ants are going to instantly pick up on it and begin taking it in the hill right away. It'll only take a hour or so before the mixture will be completely taken in and you don't have to worry about it anymore.

Summary

So there you have it two ways to get rid of those annoying ants that can ruin a good yard. Either way will work and both are cheap and easy solutions. Let us know in the comments if you have any homemade solutions to getting rid of those pesky ants.

How To Edge Your Brevard Garden With Bricks

Using brick pavers to edge your Brevard garden is a great way to dress up your garden and give it a clear distinction from your lawn. They look great are affordable and can really change the way your lawn looks.

While there are many ways to edge your garden I can think of few (if any) that are as nice as a row of brick pavers. They really look good and help to make your Brevard garden and everything in it really stand out and pop.

Here's how to install your own brick pavers around your garden for a nice clean edge.

Step #1 – Measure The Edging

The first thing you are going to want to do is grab a long rope. Then you are going to place one end of the rope at the beginning of the edge around your garden. You will then place the rest of the rope around the garden making an outline of the edge.

Then mark off with a permanent marker where the edging ends. You will then lay the rope out and measure it with a measuring tape to find out what the total length of your garden edge is and therefore how many bricks you are going to need.

The rope allows for the natural contours and curves of your lawn to be measured accurately. Once you have that measurement you are going to divide it by the length of the bricks you will be using to figure out how many you need (always add on a little extra just in case).

Step #2 – Dig A Trench

The next thing you are going to have to do is to dig a "trench" to fill with paver base. What you want to do is dig a trench around your garden edge that will fit the paver base and bricks themselves. How deep you dig is going to depend on how large the bricks you selected are.

Dig the trench with a shovel and add a two to three inches for paver base in addition to however tall the bricks are. Try to make the trench as level as possible so there won't be any irregularities in the bricks that you lay down.

Step #3 – Lay The Paver Base

You are going to want to lay two to three inches of paver base into the trench to put the pavers on. There are other things you can add in stone dust and cement for added "stickiness" of the pavers. Though you want to add another three inches to the trench to add this. Make sure that the paver base in compacted down. Then you are going to want to start laying the bricks.

Step #4 – Look For Curves

Once you have your measurements go ahead and get the bricks. Now you are going to look for curves in your garden edge. Line the edge of the garden with bricks, for curves you are going to have to cut bricks. Simply leave a pie slice shaped gap where the bricks don't fit evenly on your garden edge.

Place a brick on top of the gap then use a marker to mark where it meets the bricks below it, so you know how to cut it to fit it in the gap. To cut this you will want a circular saw with a segmented diamond blade. Cut it along the lines you drew so that it'll fit in the gap.

Step #5 – Fill In Gaps With Sand

The next thing you want to do is make sure the bricks are lying flush with one another by using a level. Dig out or add paver base as needed. Make sure all the bricks are flush against the grass line. Then you are going to fill the gaps in the bricks with polymeric sand.

Pour the sand over the bricks and then use a paintbrush to get the excess and into the gaps. Now the last thing you are going to do is water the pavers which will activate the polymeric sand locking your pavers in place.

Summary

So there you have it how to install a great looking brick paver edge around your Brevard garden. Of course if that sounded a bit complicated to you (or like too much hard work) then you can always just give us a call and we'll take care of it for you!

How To Install Landscaping Around Your Brevard Pool

One great thing about living on Florida's Space Coast is that just about any time of year you can go for a dip in your pool. While pools on their own are nice, a good landscaping job can make them even better.

With a good landscaping job you can truly change your pool into the getaway of your dreams or even just make it look a little nicer. Either way you can't go wrong with good landscaping around your pool.

Step One – Decide What You Want

What exactly are you looking for in a pool landscaping job? And is it even possible? Certain pool designs have sections already made for landscaping where you can install whatever you want even if something was already there.

For example you can replace bushes and plants (though not always easy). However if there is no spot for landscaping around your pool then you are going to have to make use with the surrounding areas (which still offer plenty of options).

For example do you want replace a patchy landscaping job with trees and beautiful flowers? Then most likely it can be done. Do you want to have the garden cleaned up and palm trees planted? Depending on the deepness of the soil also possible.

Step Two – DIY Or Hire A Professional

Then you have the option of either doing it yourself or hiring a professional (like us here at Byrd's Lawn & Landscape). If you go the DIY route be aware that what is complicated outside is going to be twice as complicated around your pool, especially if it's within the boundaries on your pool's layout.

For example planting a tree in your yard is no big deal. Planting a tree by your pool presents a number of challenges. Mostly just with maneuverability and being a pain but you also have to make sure that what you're installing can be supported. However if you know all that then it's pretty much the same process as doing the same thing outside of your pool area.

Summary

Adding landscaping to your pool is a worthy investment that looks great and helps you relax. The only issue is that it can get a little complicated and many jobs are best left up to professionals. However with a little research and hard work you can do it yourself as well.

3 Benefits Of Artificial Turf

One trend that's sweeping across America is replacing regular grass with artificial turf. Not just for pro football stadiums or government complexes but also for local businesses and residents as well. While for some the idea of walking around on artificial turf is just too weird there are a couple of reasons that everyone should consider it and why it has become so popular. Here are 3 of the best benefits for considering artificial turf in your lawn, around your house, or even select places indoors.

Artificial Turf Benefit #1 – Maintenance Free

One the artificial turf is down it is relatively maintenance free. You no longer have to do weekly upkeep such as mowing, laying sod, and worrying about your grass dying from the environment or people driving on it. With artificial turf all you have to do is set it down and forget about it. You may need to sweep it every now and then but that's it. Imagine instead of spending every weekend mowing instead spending it doing something you enjoy.

Artificial Turf Benefit #2 – Save Money

While artificial turf costs more in the beginning to install compared to sod, over the long run you save tons of money. Between not having to pay for weekly lawn service (or not having to spend time mowing it yourself and paying for gas for your mower), never having to fertilize, and never having to resod or worry about fixing bald patches you save lots of money over time. And that's not even counting the time you'll save not having to work on your lawn to keep it looking great year round. The Artificial turf that is out today can last up to 10 to 15 years before needing to be replaced. So if you sit down and do the math you will save thousands over the span of 10 years by switching to artificial grass.

Artificial Turf Benefit #3 – Worry Free Use Of Lawn

Do you dread having BBQs or parties in your lawn for fear of it getting ruined? What about people parking in the front tearing up the grass and leaving deep dark marks all across your lawn? And what about having sod lain down but it never turning out exactly how it looked in the picture? With artificial turf you don't have to worry about any of these things. It's durable enough to withstand high traffic without getting torn up and will look exactly how you wanted for years.

Overall artificial turf has many advantages over traditional grass. While it is more expensive at first its an investment in your lawn and home overall. Making artificial turf something every homeowner should at least consider.

How To Get Your Yard Ready For A Hurricane

With Hurricane Irma having recently caused havoc all across Florida many have hurricane preparedness at top of mind. There are many things you can do to your home to prepare for a hurricane such as board up your windows or even better having hurricane shutters installed. Bundling up valuables to keep them safe from water and making evacuation plans well in advance. However while many take care of what's inside their home as well as the outside what's often forgotten is preparing the yard for a hurricane. Here is a quick guide to getting your yard hurricane ready.

Step #1 – Bring In Furniture & Light Pots

The first thing you want to do is bring in furniture that'll blow away in the hurricane. This includes things like lawn chairs, grills (but not the propane tank), and small knick nacks in the yard such as garden gnomes, windmills, and the like. You also want to bring in small potted plants that'll be projectiles when the strong winds hit. With pool furniture you can save valuable room by sinking it in your pool where it'll be safe from the winds.

Step #2 – Do NOT Cut Down Tree Branches Right Before The Storm

Now naturally you're probably thinking that it'll be smart to cut down any loose branches on trees right before the hurricane comes to prevent it from breaking off during the winds but this is not a good idea. At the beginning of hurricane season is when you should have your trees trimmed not when the storm is approaching. If you get your branches cut down right before all you have done is put a bunch of dangerous projectiles in your yard that'll end up all over the place when the winds hit. Get your trees trimmed at the start of hurricane season not when a storm is coming when it's already too late.

Step #3 – Dig Trenches If Needed

If your house is prone to flooding as many in Florida are you may need to a dig a trench in certain areas. Trust me to minor damage to your yard is worth it. Laying down some sod and filling it in with some dirt is well worth not having your home flooded. Look for areas where water pools that are near to your home and dig trenches out to lower areas so the water has a place to flood. You can also reinforce around your home with sand bags if needed.

Follow these three steps will help ensure that your home is hurricane ready come hurricane season.

3 Tips To Having The Perfect Lawn

Everyone wants to have a perfect lawn. But it can be hard when you're not sure how to get a perfect lawn. Sure every product out there says that it'll make your lawn exactly the way you want it but things rarely turn out how they're promised in most advertising. However there are things you can do to make sure that you don't have to rely on products or luck to have a great looking lawn year round.

Perfect Lawn Tip #1 – Let Your Grass Grow Higher

We've talked about not cutting off too much grass at one time before but something else that's important for having a healthy lawn is that if you grass is very low allowing it time to grow up. This will do a couple of things. One it'll allow the grass to grow strong and healthy as well as prevent weeds from growing. That way your lawn will be one long strip of healthy green grass instead of pockets of grass with bald spots and weeds everywhere.

Perfect Lawn Tip #2 – Use Quality Grass

While most are fans of Bahia grass because it's cheap and you can cover a large area with it the truth of the matter is you'll never have a truly great looking lawn with cheap grass. St. Augustine is a great grass that while more expensive then Bahia is of much higher quality and will be reflected in how your lawn looks. Bahia no matter what might look a little patchy and not like a lawn you'll see in the magazines. Use a quality grass it's worth it in the long run.

Perfect Lawn Tip #3 – Use Professionals

We're called professionals for a reason. When you want something done right you call in a professional. This applies to everything from getting in your best shape through using a personal trainer to getting a perfect lawn using qualified professionals. When looking for a good lawn company you want someone with lots of good reviews, is community based (not a faceless giant), and that has been around for at least a couple of years.

Follow these three tips and you'll be well on your way to having the perfect lawn that'll be the envy of all your neighbors.

How To Fix An Ugly Lawn

So you're lawn isn't looking how you wanted as a matter of fact if you're being honest, it's downright ugly. You're not sure what happened between what you envisioned in your head and what is in your yard but something happened and it wasn't good. No problem getting your lawn in great shape is a full time job (it is after all how I make my living).

But even if you don't have that much time to work on your yard to get it in tip top shape (and who does?) there are still many things you can do to fix that ugly lawn that you can do in your spare time. Of course that easiest option is to simply hire a professional and be done with it but I know many enjoy working on their lawn and take pride in doing the work themselves. I'm like this myself so I understand so let's get started.

The Mower You Use

Believe it or not but the mower that you use has a big impact on the health of your yard. Now by mower I don't mean riding versus push or anything like that. Rather I'm talking about the condition of your mower, mainly your blades. Most people think that they're blades can be sharpened once or twice a year and they'll be good to go but that isn't the case. You need to keep your blades sharp year round sharpening them 4-5 times and anytime you hit a large rock or stick that will damage the blade.

A Quality Fertilizer

There are all kinds of fertilizers that you can use out there. Some are very expensive and some are very cheap. I've found that for the most part you get what you pay for when it comes to fertilizers. You don't have to spring for a the highest priced one but look for one on the higher end to be safe. Look for the three numbers on front of the bag and only buy fertilizer that is 8-8-8 or higher. Don't overdo it with fertilizer you don't want to fry your lawn use the calculations I laid out previously in the fertilizer chapter and you'll be safe.

Kill The Weeds

There are a couple of options here for getting rid of your weeds. There are many products you can use to kill the weeds. There are benefits and drawbacks to using chemicals to kill weeds as opposed to pulling or tilling them. With chemicals you risk hurting the grass as well as the weeds and should only be used on areas with lots of weeds or near the house. You should manually pull the weeds in areas with few weeds and where grass is growing. If you do not feel up to doing this task yourself there are many professional weed spraying companies in the area that can do it for you.

Following these tips will help transform your ugly lawn into a lawn you can be proud of with just a little bit of work.

How To Keep Your St. Augustine Grass Healthy Year Round

St. Augustine grass when properly taken care of is some of the most beautiful grass that you can have in Florida. It has a nice green healthy look that is great for model homes, commercial properties, and your own backyard. However if not taken care of properly you can run into trouble and end up with patches of dead grass which no matter what kind they are don't look good. So here are some tips to making sure your St.

Augustine grass stays in tip top shape year round.

Mow At A Higher Level

I've talked about making sure you let you grass grow a couple of inches and making sure to not mow it down to the roots every time to make sure it grows healthy and this holds doubly true for St. Augustine grass. Make sure you let your St. Augustine grass grow to at least 3-4 inches and don't cut more than an inch off when you're mowing. Doing so can kill the grass as well as leave it more susceptible to disease and bugs. When we mow St Augustine grass we usually keep our mower decks to a height of 4 to 4 1/2. Keeping the deck high allows for the grass to grow and thicken up more.

Don't Overwater

While it may seem like a bigger threat would be under watering that's not always the case especially when we have strong rains like we frequently get here on the Space Coast. Overwatering can lead to development of fungus in the lawn. You only want to use about 1 inch of water per week (from sprinklers or from rain) during the summer and spring months. Never run the system during the middle of the day also. Must be ran in the morning or evening when there is no direct sunlight so the sun does not burn the wet grass. I do not recommend running the system during the night also because standing water can lead to fungus and root rot which will only hurt your grass.

Following these two tips will help ensure that your St. Augustine lawn stays healthy and green all year round.

How To Keep Your Lawn Green During The Hot Summer Months

During the hot summer months your yard can get damaged from the hot sun if not taken care of properly. Especially here in Brevard where the summers can be particularly intense. However there is a way that you can keep your lawn green all summer long. It doesn't take that much work once set up and much of it will be common sense by now if you've read everything I've written so far. But it's always good to go back over the basics especially when it comes to keeping your lawn healthy and green all year long.

Keep Your Grass Long

So many people cut their grass way to short (and this includes lawn companies that don't know what they're doing). You should let your grass grow a couple of inches during the summer and should never be cut below one inch especially when it's hot. The longer the grass is the more resilient and healthy it's going to be. Letting your grass grow to a couple of inches in height will keep it from withering away under the hot summer sun.

Water Consistently

You need to make sure that not only are you watering on a consistent basis (but not over watering) but also that you sprinklers are hitting all of your yard. You can get brown spots if your sprinklers aren't set up properly and you're not getting adequate yard coverage. It's always good to test out your sprinklers and make sure they're all working and that your entire yard is getting covered not just patches of it. This is especially important during the high heat of the summer and during periods where there is little rain.

Keep Your Grass Green Year Round

These two simple tips are easy but they're also very effective. You'd be surprised how many yards end up with damage during the summer because of ignoring either one or both of these tips. Keep them both in mind during the summer months to keep your grass green year round.

How To Save Your Lawn From Heat Stress

Heat stress can spell trouble for your lawn. Leading to dead grass, brown spots, and eventually having to resod or lay seed in hopes of getting your grass green again. However there is a way to keep your lawn from suffering the ill effects of heat stress that I'm going to show you here. I should note that lawns are particularly vulnerable to heat stress here on Florida's Space Coast because of the hot summers (and sometimes spring and falls as well). So to prevent your lawn from looking like a patchy dried up mess listen up.

Heavy Watering On Certain Spots

Alright now you don't want to overwater your lawn as that won't help it but there are certain times when it may be good to overwater certain dry spots of your lawn to get it back to full health. Again this isn't meant to be done as a long term strategy but only if your lawn starts to look a little worn down by the heat. Which during the hot summer months is a very likely possibility. You want to water a full inch one day and then up to another inch the day after. After this continue your normal watering schedule.

What If It Rains?

A natural question is if it starts to rain how should I adjust? One thing you'll want to do is get a rain gauge so you can tell how much water your lawn is getting and then be able to adjust accordingly. Also keep in mind that if it's particularly hot out that some of the water out of your rain gauge may evaporate so you'll want to adjust for that. Preventing the negative effects of heat stress comes down to keeping a well watered lawn. During times with little rain but high temperatures hit your lawn with what's proscribed here when you start seeing brown spots or dull grass to get it back to full health and color.

3 Tips For A Lush Green Lawn

Everyone wants a lush green lawn but yet except for a lucky few most end up with a lawn that has that true healthy green look. However it doesn't have to be this way. The reasons for having a lawn that is in poor health and losing it's dark green color are mostly preventable and with a few simple tips can be fixed. Here are 3 of the best tips to help you get the lush green lawn that you've always wanted.

Lush Green Lawn Tip #1 – Use Sharpened Mower Blades

I've talked about this before but it bears mentioning again. If you don't sharpen your mower blades you'll end up damaging your grass even when cutting it to the right height. What happens is the blunted blades tear up the grass instead of cutting it cleanly. Imagine trying to hack through something with a dull ax versus a sharpened one. The dull one is going to cause more overall trauma while the sharpened one will cut cleanly through.

Lush Green Lawn Tip #2 – Mow To The Right Height

Most of us mow weekly regardless if our grass needs it or not. That means our grass can take a beating and get cut down when its trying to heal and recover. You should never mow more than an inch or 1/3 of a grass's height at one time. And you'll want to keep your grass at least two inches high. So if your grass is not this height skip mowing that day/week for a healthier yard.

Lush Green Lawn Tip #3 – Water Properly

Watering properly covers a couple basic steps. It means one that you're giving your yard enough water week to week so that it can grow. Not only do you need to get the amount right but make sure your sprinklers are properly placed and that water is getting to every corner of your lawn. Even properly placed sprinklers can have trouble if there's something blocking the path of the water or they have a unusual propulsion stream. Something to watch out for.

Following the above 3 tips will keep your lawn lush and green all year round.

What Is Summer Dormancy & Why Does It Matter?

Sometimes your lawn getting brown isn't as bad as you think, particularly during the hot summer months when your lawn can go into something called summer dormancy. Summer dormancy is when your lawn may turn a shade of brown but it's not because it's dead by rather it's going into summer dormancy. It's caused by cells with the grass that are responding to the summer conditions. it's a survival mechanism and meant to protect your grass.

What To Do When Your Lawn Goes Dormant

Summer dormancy can be caused by high temperatures for prolonged periods of time, excessive dryness such as during drought, and longer days where your grass is exposed to sun for a much longer period of time then during the winter, fall, and spring months. It's not a big deal and your grass will not grow during dormancy as it's saving all it's nutrients for when there are better conditions and more rainfall.

Sort of like how other animals will store up for the winter your grass stores up for the summer in a way. Now if this bothers you and you have particularly brown spots on your lawn that are an eyesore then you can bring your lawn out of dormancy by frequently watering it. With enough water the grass will come out of dormancy and start growing and getting green again.

Does It Matter?

Yes and no. It matters in one way because it shows your grass is responding to the environment and in need of more water if you want a lush green lawn. So from a purely aesthetic standpoint yes it does matter for a lush green lawn. Now from a purely survival standpoint (of your grass of course) it doesn't matter. It'll be fine and come back to growth once the season changes so it's nothing to get too worked up over. Just a natural survival mechanism.

Can You Paint Your Lawn Green?

Don't laugh, it's a growing trend. Instead of worrying about watering, the heat, and other concerns many are instead opting to simply paint their lawns green instead of doing all the hard work that is required to do so naturally. And surprisingly it's safe for both pets and kids. The first I heard of it was from a guy in Sacramento who started a company during drought time that painted people's lawns green.

Painting Your Lawn

This is something that you can do yourself or have a professional do. You can order the paint online. It's a specialized paint that's not only non toxic but also safe for the environment. Now this isn't paint you'll get from your local hardware store (at least not yet, as the trend grows this may change) it's a special paint designed directly for use on your grass. EnviroColor is an prime example of this type of paint.

After you buy the paint all you need is a sprayer and some time to go around your lawn literally coloring it green. It doesn't matter how dry or brown your lawn is when you're simply coloring it in it'll be as green as you want it to be no matter what. Just make sure to be careful around plants and areas that you don't want painted. But other than that paint away.

Is This The Future?

So is this the future? Instead of worrying about keeping your grass green the natural way instead just painting it green whenever it gets brown? We're not sure yet. This is a growing trend and especially with paint that is not only safe for animals and kids but also for the environment. Combine that with less work and personalized coloring (different shades of green and even reds and browns for pine straw and the like) and this is something that will only grow as time goes on.

Also opens up lots of options for holiday and celebration designs on your yard. We've seen everything from the American flag to NFL logos and who knows what else will come up.

Is Your Grass Dead Or Just Dormant?

So you're looking out at your lawn and it's brown. You think no big deal it's summer after all and I just read all about summer dormancy but then you wonder what if it's not dormant but rather dead? How can you tell? Is there a test you can do? And how long can grass stay dormant before dying? Here's the thing as long as the crown is healthy then your grass is going to come back. But if something happens to the crown then your grass is dead.

So instead of pulling up a section of your grass and checking the crown is there something else that you can do to see if your lawn is truly dormant or actually dead? Yes there is and I'm going to share it with you here.

The Tug Test

The first thing that you want to do is try the "tug test" all the tug test is going out to your lawn and yanking on a chunk of grass. If it rips right up then it's a good bet that your grass is dead instead of just dormant. That means you'll have to reseed or resod. However the tug test obviously isn't the most scientific test there is. After all some are particularly strong and will rip up healthy grass and other times you may just have hit a soft spot so there are other methods to testing if your lawn is dormant or dead.

The Water Test

The next thing to do is test to see if it's dormant by doing what you'd do to fix a dormant yard. And that is to water it heavily and give it some time to see if it starts coming back. You have to be patient with this because even with watering it's not going to spring back to full green right away. Now if after watering for a couple of weeks you can't see a difference then it's a good bet that your lawn is dead and not dormant.

3 Things To Look For In A Lawn Company

There are plenty of options to choose from when it comes to lawn care. Lawn care companies are relatively easy to start and especially in Brevard everyone knows someone who owns or operates one. However quantity does not translate to quality and you need to be careful who you choose for your lawn service and landscaping needs. There are plenty of charlatans out there who perform shoddy work and are unprofessional.

Here are 3 key things that you are going to want to look out for when choosing a lawn care or landscaping company. While there are more things that you can look for these 3 will help you filter out those that are unprofessional and could cheat you or do work that will need to be redone or at best not be what you wanted.

Lawn Company Must Have #1 – Testimonials

The more testimonials that a lawn care or landscaping company has the more likely they'll provide what you want. Not just testimonials but testimonials stretching back through the years you want testimonials that are frequent as well as many things change and the company could have changed hands or have different crews. A company with lots of up to date testimonials is a good sign that they'll give you what they want.

Lawn Company Must Have #2 – Equipment

Are they a professional lawn service company with top of the line equipment such as Scag mowers? Or are they pretenders loading up their dads lawn mower in the back of their truck? The equipment that is used on your lawn makes a huge differences. This is why professional lawn companies will put down thousands of dollars on a mower because they know how big of a difference that it makes when it comes to getting your yard to look its best.

Lawn Company Must Have #3 – Customer Service

Can you talk directly to the owner? Is it his phone number on the website or a phone number of an receptionist who will redirect you or even worse someone he outsourced from another country. It's important to be able to communicate and form a relationship with the owner and be treated as a valued customer or even a friend instead of just another number.

Using these 3 guidelines to help filter through the lawn and landscaping companies will ensure you end up with one that is professional and will get you the results that you want.

How Much Does A Good Landscaping Job Add To The Value Of Your Home?

We all know that how our yard and landscaping looks plays a part in the value of our home and how it's perceived by others. Like it or not humans are very visual people it may not be fair but we judge books by their cover. This includes when looking at a home. Even if it's a nice house in a nice location having shoddy landscape or dead grass is going to really hurt one's first impression of the home and reflect how they feel about it.

Imagine someone showing up for a job interview that was professional dressed, 15 minutes early, answered all your questions perfectly, but then you noticed half of their teeth were rotten. Even though it's not fair it's very unlikely that person would get the job. Little things can add up big time and lawn and landscaping is no exception.

How Much Value Can Quality Lawn & Landscaping Add To The Value Of Your Home?

The common estimate is that a well done landscaping job can add around 15% value to the house. But there are some issues with that. First off understand that the value of your home is largely about perception. Of course the neighborhood you live in, the quality of your home, and how good the real estate agent is all play a huge role but how your home is perceived makes a big difference as well.

A good landscaping job can make an ordinary boring home that would only command market value or less turn into something completely different. It can make a normal house into a lush tropical getaway with the addition of some tropical plants and water works. Or it can turn a average suburb house into a home with a place for scenic picnics and your family to gather. Perception is everything in marketing.

Meaning that it's not going to be known how much value landscaping actually adds to your home. And 15% can be on the low end. That's why it's important to have quality landscaping not only if you're selling your home but just for the enjoyment of it as well.

The Difference Between Perennial & Annual Plants

When deciding how you want to do your landscaping one thing that's important to keep in mind is if you want to use perennial or annual plants and the differences between them. They both have their pros and cons and a complete landscaping job can include some of each if done right. However before getting into it, it's important to know what the difference is between them.

Perennial Plants

Perennial plants are generally favored as far as convenience goes. Perennial plants are those that when taken care of properly continue to grow year after year. They go dormant in the winter when it gets cold and then come back in the spring. You don't have to replace them year to year. They are generally a bit most costly then annual plants but that's because of the longer life and convenience of not having to replace them every year. However there some benefits for annual plants as well.

Annual Plants

Annual plants are those that only last a year and die in winter. While at first this may seem to make perennials the hands down winner and superior it's not that simple. First off annual plants are a bit cheaper then perennials on average and in addition to that they tend to be more colorful and more aesthetically pleasing. But you also have to rework the soil and replant annuals.

Using Both

Perennials can also take a year or two to bloom and when they do will generally not be as bright or colorful as the annuals. Because of this it pays to have both used in your landscaping scheme to add color and convenience to your landscaping making it beautiful during the summer, spring, and fall months. Neither one is best and certain people may prefer the convenience of a landscape made up of all perennials while others may like the beauty of a landscape made up of all annuals. It's up to you to find what you want.

The Importance Of Using Native Plants In Your Landscaping

There is a variety of things that you can do with your landscaping. Many different exotic effects and choices. However one thing that you always want to keep in mind is the importance of using native plants in your landscaping. Meaning here in the Melbourne, Florida area you want to use plants that are native to central Florida in your landscaping.

First I'll address why they matter for your yard and how it looks. Then I'll get into some other reasons that using native plants is important for your yard for reasons other than how it looks. This isn't to say you can never use any other type of plant just using what's correct for where you live has many benefits and that the majority of your landscaping should always be done with native plants.

Native Plants For Beautiful Landscaping

The first benefit of using native plants is that they'll naturally blend in with your landscaping. And by blend in I don't mean look boring but rather will look natural and add to your overall landscaping. It'll go with your grass and what's naturally growing adding to the aesthetics of your landscaping. Sort of like putting a nice mahogany desk in a nice office filled with wood. But that same desk would look weird in an office filled with plastic chairs and work spaces. Native plants also have the added benefit of being lower maintenance and in particular requiring less water.

Helping The Environment

As an added bonus adding in native plants can also help the native lands. By either restoring plants that have been overtaken by foreign plants as well as give native species a place to live and thrive. Whether it's birds or other animals. Using native plants will not only add to the beauty of your landscape but also help with the native wild life and preservation efforts. Making them a much desired part of every landscape.

3 Ways To Increase The Curb Appeal Of Your House

Curb appeal is important to many of us. We always want our homes to look the best because we take pride in the way our home and landscaping looks. However most of us would be happy with even a little more curb appeal. So we're going to look into 3 ways in which you can increase the curb appeal of your home. They're all going to require some work but are well worth it in the end. So if you're looking to increase the curb appeal, look, and value of your home then be sure to keep reading.

Increase Curb Appeal Method #1 – Installing Shrubs To An Empty Bed

Having a layer of dirt or mulch with nothing but a few weeds around your house doesn't help with its curb appeal. While you don't have to get crazy fancy with ways to dress it up installing some shrubs or bushes could be just what you need. A few shrubs can change a dirt or mulch patch from looking cheap and worn down to a professional landscaping job that'll be guaranteed to raise your curb appeal.

Increase Curb Appeal Method #2 – Lay New Mulch

Freshly lain mulch looks great. It has a nice rich color that really adds to your landscaping and looks good. However with time your mulch will eventually lose its color and have to be replaced. A fresh mulch job on a yard is like putting a fresh new coat of paint on a house. Plus not only does it make the landscaping job look better but it's good for your plants as well.

Increase Curb Appeal Method #3 – Trim Your Trees

I know when I think of curb appeal the first thing I'm thinking of has to do with landscaping however making sure your trees aren't overgrown and blocking parts of your home can really help increase your curb appeal. Overgrown branches not only represent a potential safety hazard (especially come hurricane season) but also don't look good. Getting old worn out or overgrown branches taken care of can really change the way your home looks.

So there it is. 3 ways to increase the curb appeal of your home that are simple and not too hard to do.

How To Trim Your Hedges The Right Way

There isn't much that looks quite as clean as a nice freshly cut row of hedges. While anyone can go out there and just whack off a certain amount of green until things are relatively even that's not the way to get the most out of your hedges or keep them healthy. There is a right way and a wrong way to trim your hedges and here I'm going to tell you about the right way to do it. The right way will not only make sure that your hedges stay looking good year round but also that they stay healthy and keep coming back.

When To Cut

During particularly raining seasons your hedges are going to grow more than in seasons with less rain. This is obvious and it's during this season that you'll have to keep up on your hedges to keep them from getting out of hand. When you start to notice lots of water shoots (single long pieces of your hedge sticking up) is when you'll want to trim your hedge.

The first thing you want to do is get rid of the water shoots. All you have to do with this is simply tear them off. They stick out pretty far so this will be relatively easy. The next is to cut back the hedge a little bit on the top or anywhere else it's growing over. Not a ton you just want to snip off a inch or so. One key with keeping your plants healthy no matter what they are is no tearing them apart but rather trimming them back little by little.

Don't take off to much as this can damage your hedge and lead to infection, disease, bugs moving in, or the hedge dying none of these are good so make sure you only take off a little at a time. Even if they're particularly overgrown just take it little by little eventually over time you'll have clean cut hedges.

That's How It's Done

Keep the above in mind next time you trim your hedges. Hedges like anything else can get damaged when not properly trimmed. Make sure to not take off too much at one time and to do so gently. You can always come back a few days or even a week later and cut off a little more if you have to. Little by little you'll shape your hedges to the way that you want.

Sod Vs. Seed: Which Is Better?

So you have a brown or bald spot on your lawn and want to fix it. Let's say you've tried bringing it back to life by watering it, making sure you don't cut it too short, as well as threw some fertilizer on it and still nothing's happening. The grass is dead and it isn't coming back. So now it's time to replace it, you have two options. You can either use sod or have it seeded both have their pros and cons which will be discussed here.

Laying Down Sod

One great benefit of sod is that you got nearly full grown grass there right away. Sure you'll have to water it quite frequently so it takes but once sod is put down it's generally going to stay there. It's less vulnerable then seeding but it also comes with its drawbacks. For on sod is a lot harder to put down than seeds. It's also going to cost you a little more. To make sure that your sod is done right and is going to take I always recommend going with a professional. You can do it yourself just make sure that it gets plenty of water and is set down properly.

Seeding The Dead Spots

Now we'll look at seeding and it's pros and cons. With seeding it's relatively labor free. Unless you count spreading some seeds across the yard as labor. You'll want to make sure the ground is prepared to take the seed at first and then afterwards are going to have to water it very frequently so the seeds can take root and grow into healthy green grass. Seeds take less labor to throw down then sod and they're also cheaper. But they're also much more vulnerable than sod. Not only do you have to water it frequently but you also have to monitor it for weeds to make sure they don't take root.

Overall it really depends on what you want. If you don't mind getting your hands dirty or paying someone else to do so and have some change then sod is your number one choice. But if you're on a tight budget and don't want to lug around sod then seed is a great option for you.

3 Ways To Make Use Of Grass Clippings

Most consider grass clippings to be a annoyance. A garbage item that has to be bagged up and disposed of. But there are actually many uses that you can use grass clipping for instead of just getting rid of them. So before you decide to dispose of your grass clippings next time you mow here are 3 neat things that you can do to make use of those grass clippings.

Grass Clipping Use #1 – Use For Compost

Grass clippings can be great for use in your compost pile. Combine that with some dry leaves or paper and you'll have a potent combination. Just make sure to mix it up good so that it combines with whatever you're mixing it with. It's good to get a mix going with your compost pile. You can also throw things like egg shells, banana peels, apple cores, and coffee grounds in there to make a even more potent pile.

Grass Clipping Use #2 – Just Leave Them

Although this doesn't look the best but leaving your grass clippings on the lawn can help your grass grow and be healthy. Being organic matter the grass clippings are going to break down and turn into minerals that the grass can then use (or reuse more like it) for growth. As a matter of fact for some lawns this is a must if your grass is low on minerals and isn't being fertilized. So you can use the grass clippings for a greener healthier lawn by leaving them there.

Grass Clipping Use #3 – Use Them In Your Garden

What you can also do is put down grass clippings in your garden to help your plants grow. Now you don't want to use too much, just a little goes far. This clippings will break down enriching the soil of your garden. All you want is to sprinkle the grass clipping around the base of plants in your garden. Just remember not to use too much.

So there you have it 3 uses for grass clippings to help enrich your lawn!

How To Plant Palm Trees

Palm trees are some of the most iconic tropical trees that there is. Nothing says the tropics or relaxation like a yard filled with palm trees. A palm tree can be exactly what you need to turn your backyard into the tropical paradise that you've always wanted. Melbourne, Florida has the perfect growing conditions for palm trees and they make a great addition to any yard. But in order to make sure you have a palm that'll stay healthy you have to know how to plant it right.

Step One – Dig The Hole

No surprise here digging the hole is the first step. Now different palms are going to require different depths. Some smaller palms that work more as shrubs then trees will require holes that are smaller than palms that are larger. Since there are over 2,500 different kinds of palm trees it's best to just look up what the required depth is instead of listing them all here. Just make sure to hit the right depth as too high or too low and the palm may die or fail to thrive.

Step Two – Place Palm In The Hole

You'll want to do this with someone who can help you or with professionals. This is because you want to make sure that your tree is being installed straight up otherwise it can grow at an angle. Have someone hold it where you want and check from a distance it's hard to tell from right next to it how straight it is. Then fill it in with the soil that was dug out of it.

Step Three – Water, Water, Water

The next thing you'll want to do is water it right away. Not only does this help the tree grow but it also helps the soil settle. Water it every day for at least the first week. Then check out what watering schedule is recommended for the type of palm planted. Then you can mulch it if you'd like.

And that's all there is to it. It's simple but can be work intensive. If you're worried about any of the steps or lugging the tree around and getting it set up right then use professionals who have experience with planting palm trees the right way.

How To Protect Your Plants During The Winter

Living in Florida one usually doesn't pay that much attention to keeping plants protected during the winter months. After all with no snow and most winters not getting anywhere close to freezing it can seem like worrying about plants for winter isn't something that needs to be considered. However while we aren't going to get snow any time soon temperatures can still drop enough to damage plants especially more fragile ones. There are a couple things you can do during particularly cold times to make sure your fragile tropical plants survive.

Use Coverings

The simplest but very effective method is to simply cover your plants with sheets or frost blankets. Just keep your trees covered on particularly cold nights. In Florida you won't generally have to use anything other than sheets so need to spend money on frost blankets (except maybe some places in North Florida). Just find a good sheet and cover up your tree on nights when it supposed to get cold. Mulch also helps keeps the roots from freezing but that's hardly a concern in Florida.

Keep Them In A Greenhouse

A little pricier but you may want to consider getting a greenhouse. A greenhouse will allow you to grow tropical plants year round and keep them safe from changes in temperature. One thing that's great about a greenhouse is the more plants that you put in it the warmer it's going to be and therefore the healthier your plants are going to be.

Moving all of your tropical plants into a greenhouse for winter or just keeping them there all year is another great option to keep your plants safe during cold winter months.

These two are really all you need for keeping you plants safe in Florida during the winter months. For smaller plants you can also just take them in the house during particularly cold nights as well if you don't have a greenhouse and don't feel like buying sheets for every plant in your yard.

About The Author

Sam Byrd is the owner of Byrd's Lawn & Landscape the premier lawn and landscaping service of Florida's Space Coast including areas such as Melbourne, Palm Bay, Viera, & Rockledge. Sam started the company after working at Ace Hardware with a borrowed trailer and an old worn down John Deere mower. He has since built it up to over 100 accounts and growing.

Sam has worked with both small residential yards to entire complexes. He has cleaned up after hurricanes, laid sod, installed plants, grinded stumps, trimmed trees, mowed lawns, killed weeds, and so much more all across Brevard county and enjoys every second of it.

If you're interested in working with Sam give him a call at 321-412-3006. Also you can learn more about Byrd's Lawn & Landscape at byrdslawnandlandscapefl.com.

Also if you found value in this book please leave a review, we appreciate it so much. Thanks!

Made in the USA
Columbia, SC
20 December 2019

85446566R00107